This Book Belongs To:

_____

Copyright Material

Copyright Material

Copyright Material

Copyright Material

Copyright Material

Copyright Material

Copyright Material

Copyright Material

Copyright Material

Copyright Material

Copyright Material

Copyright Material

Copyright Material

Copyright Material

Copyright Material

Copyright Material

Copyright Material

Copyright Material

Copyright Material

Copyright Material

Copyright Material

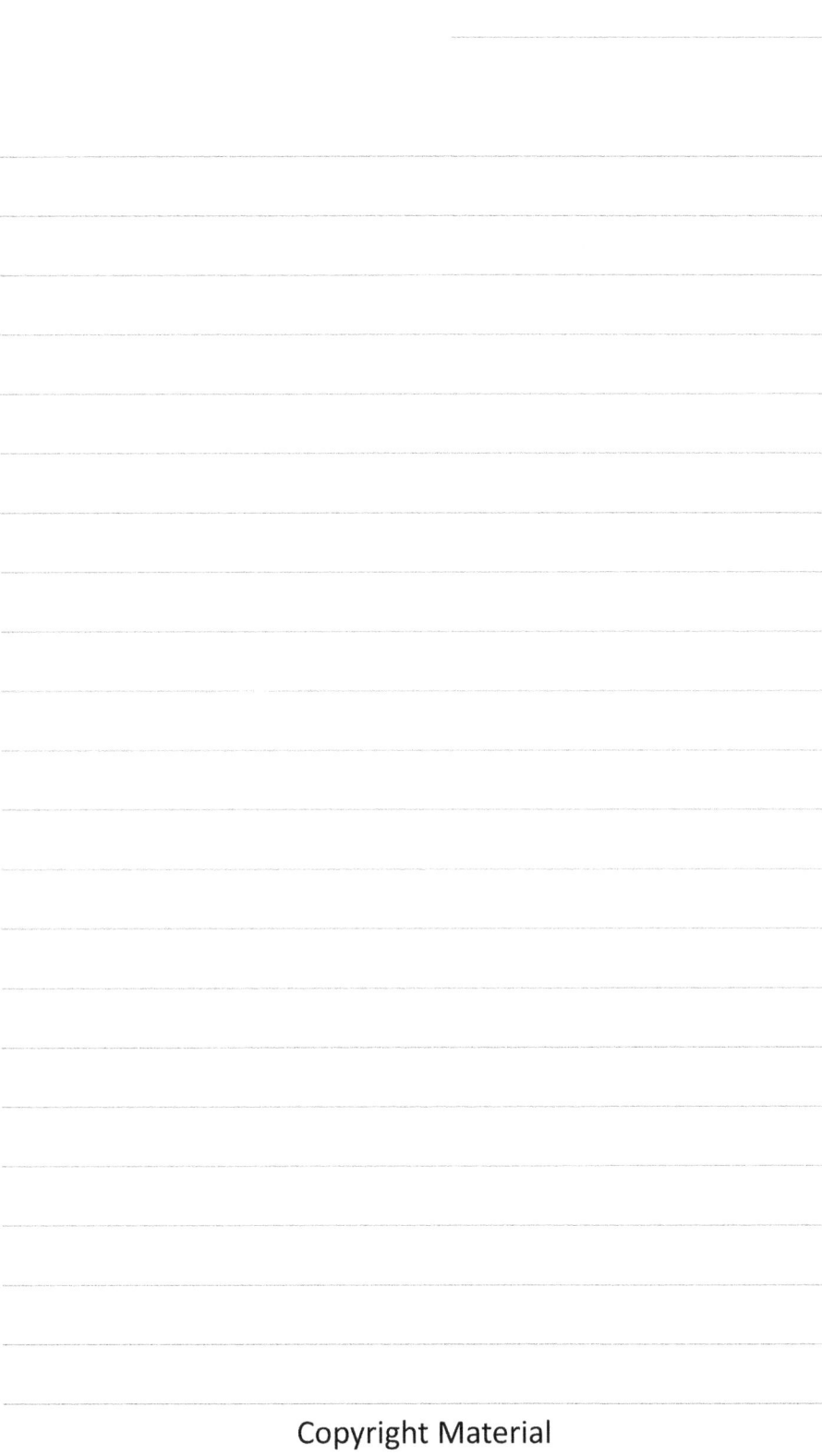

Copyright Material

Copyright Material

Copyright Material

Copyright Material

Copyright Material

Made in United States
Orlando, FL
08 December 2023